AF428958

INSTRUCTIONS

YOU NEED SCISSORS, A CUTTER (FOR SOME SMALL PARTS), RE-USABLE ADHESIVE (PATAFIX, BLU TACK...), COLORED PENCILS, AND A SMALL RIGID CARDBOARD (FOR THE SUPPORTS).

- CUT OUT THE DOLLS ON THE BACK COVER.
- CUT OUT THE CLOTHES OF YOUR CHOICE. COLOR THEM IF YOU HAVE CHOSEN CLOTHES TO COLOR.
- ADJUST THE CLOTHES ON THE DOLL.
- FOLD THE STRIPS ON THE BACK OF THE DOLL. TO MAKE THE CLOTHES FIT PERFECTLY, YOU CAN USE RE-SABLE ADHÉSIVE (BLU TAK, PATAFIX...).
- YOU CAN ALSO CHANGE THE HEAD OF YOUR DOLL!

TO MAKE THE DOLL STAND UPRIGHT, USE THE SUPPORT MODELS ON THE LAST PAGES.

- TAKE A RIGID CARDBOARD.
- CUT OUT 2 SUPPORTS USING THE TEMPLATES ON THE LAST PAGE.
- CUT A SLOT, FOLLOWING THE RED LINE OF THE MODEL.
- INSERT THE DOLL'S FEET INTO THE SLOT, AS SHOWN ON THE LAST PAGE.

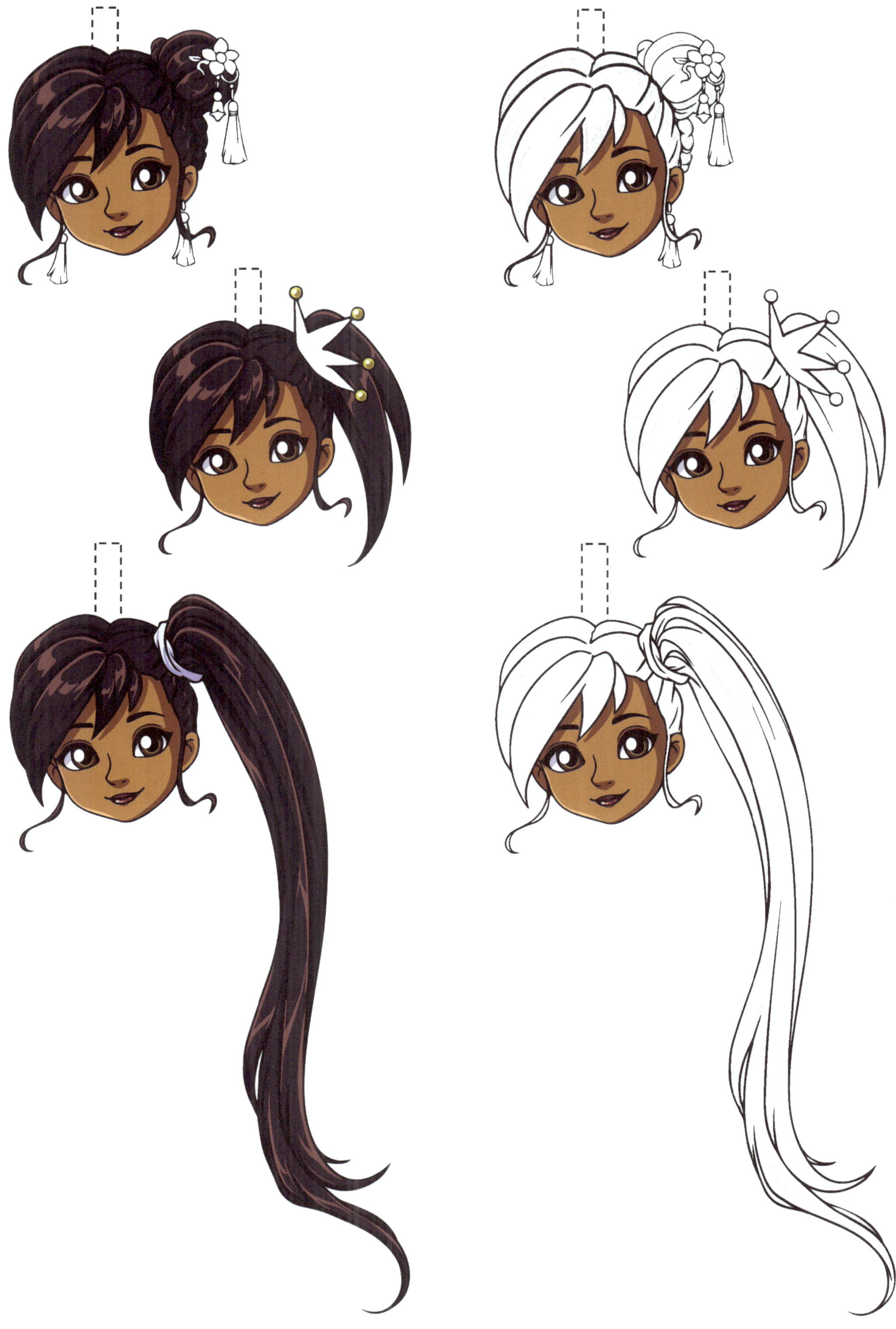

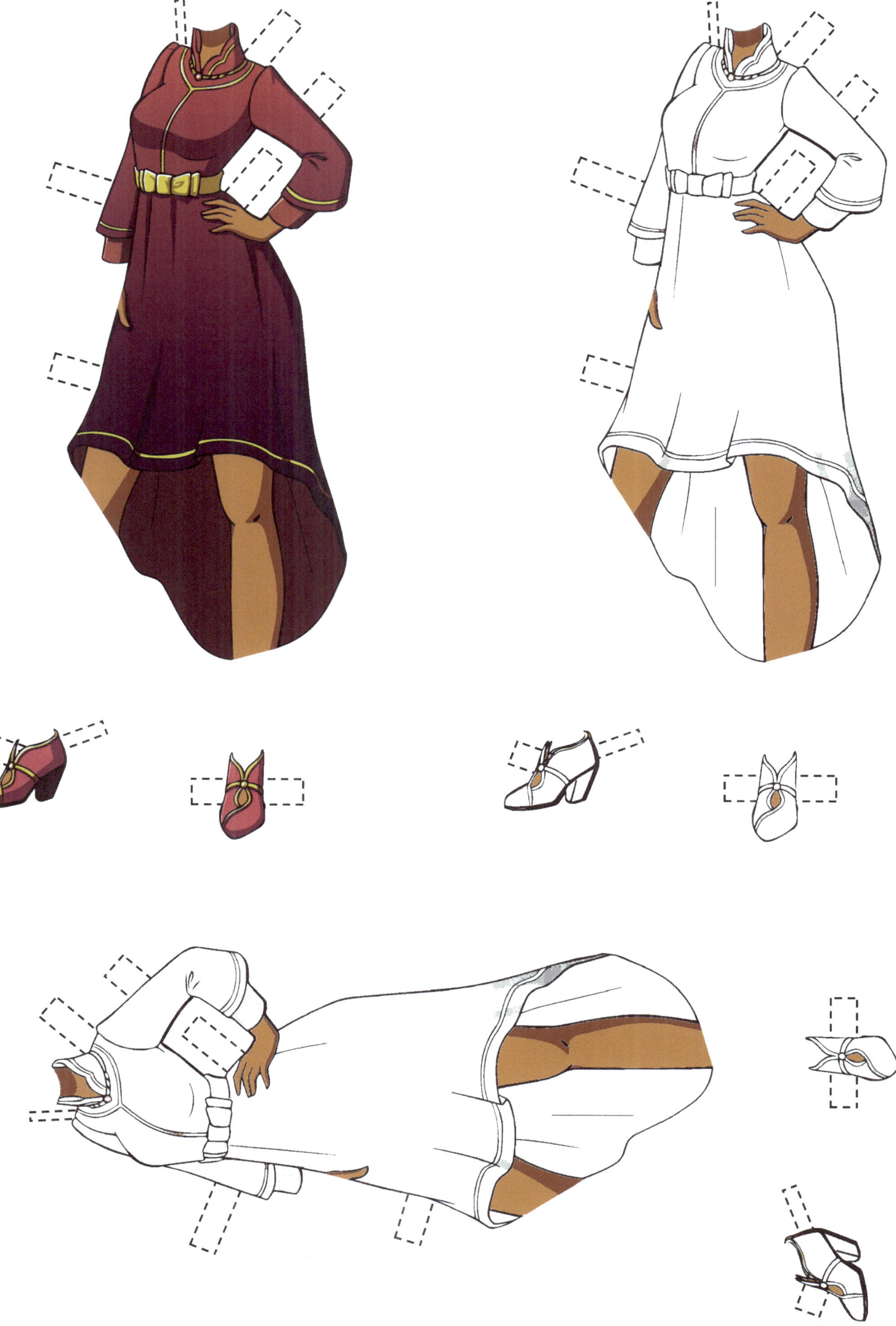

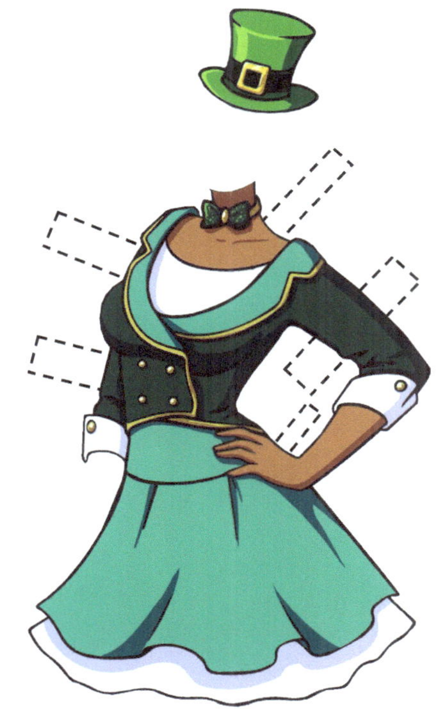

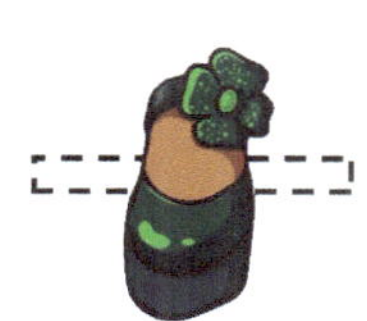

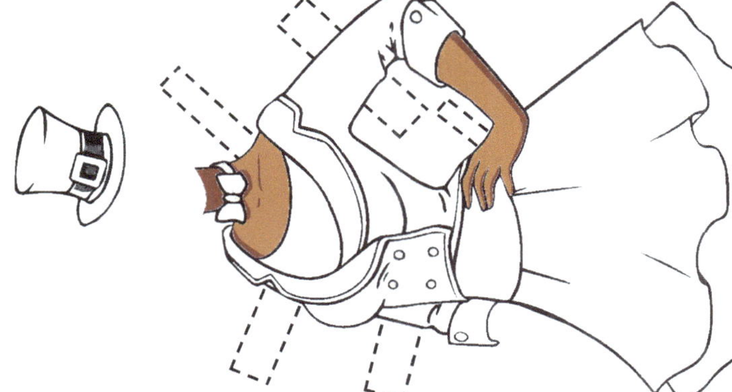
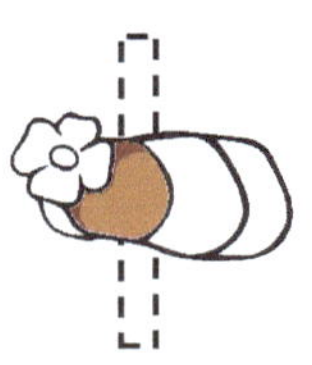
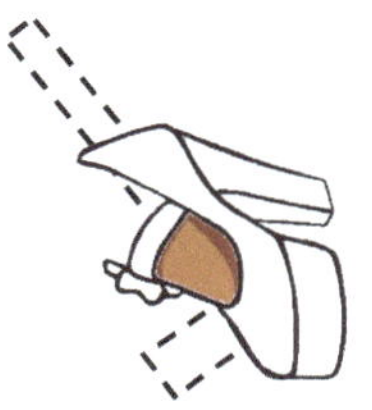

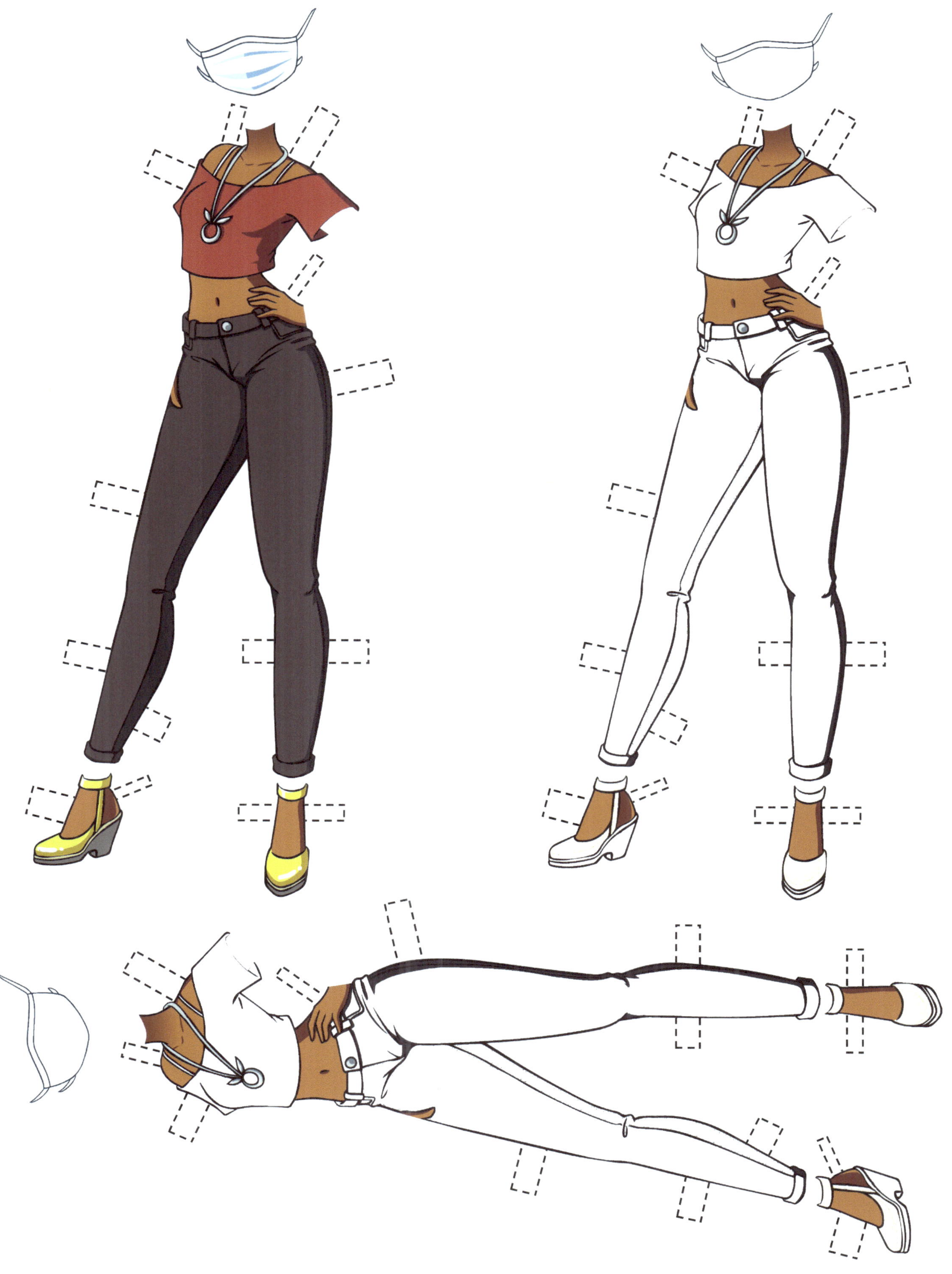

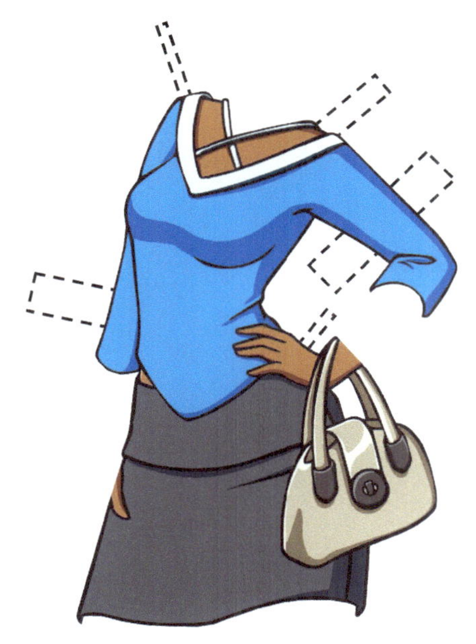

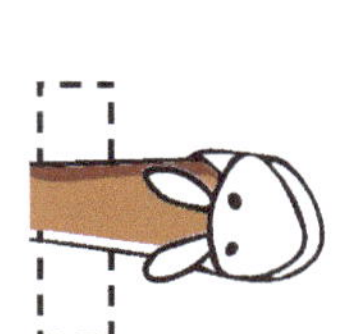

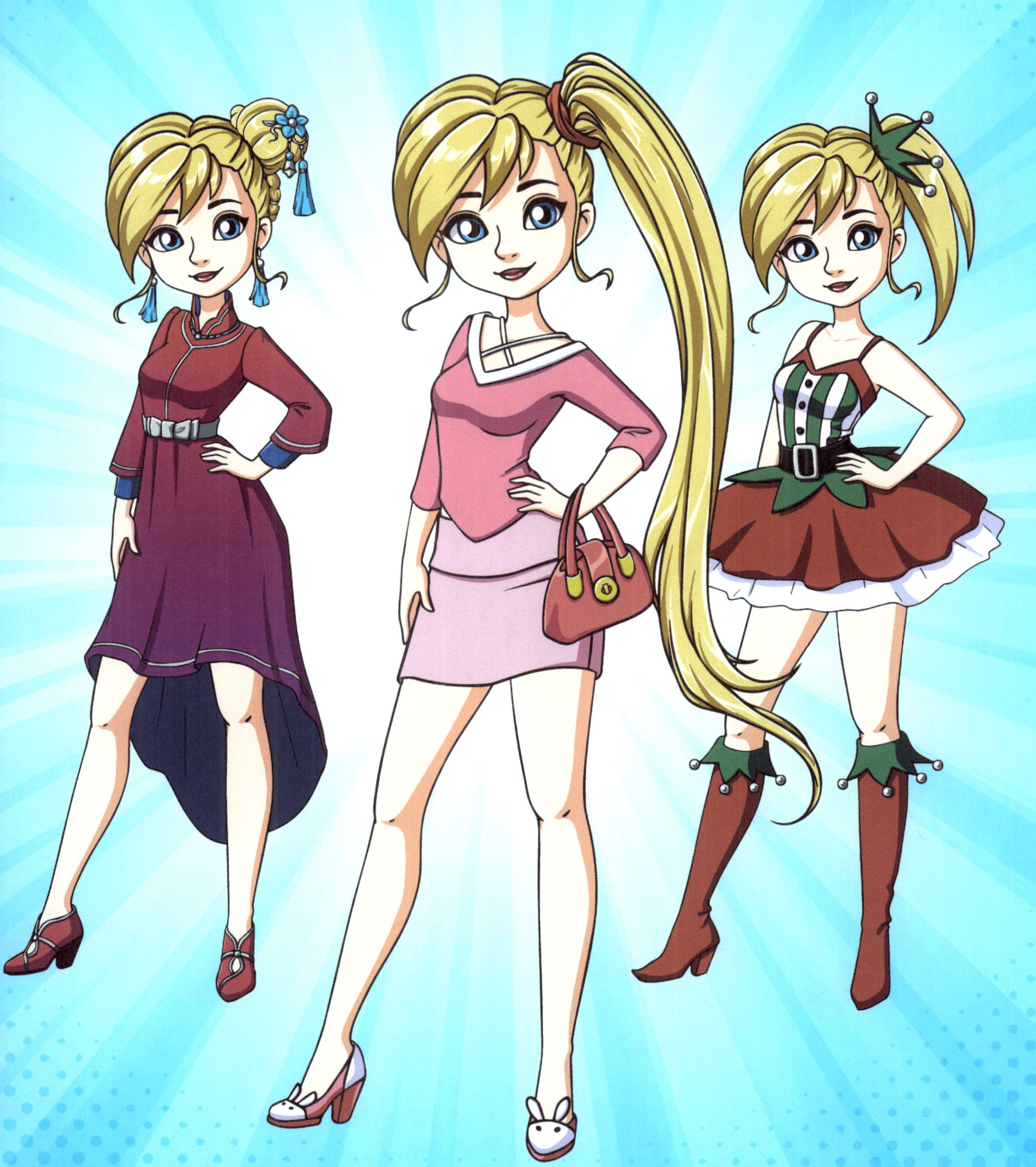

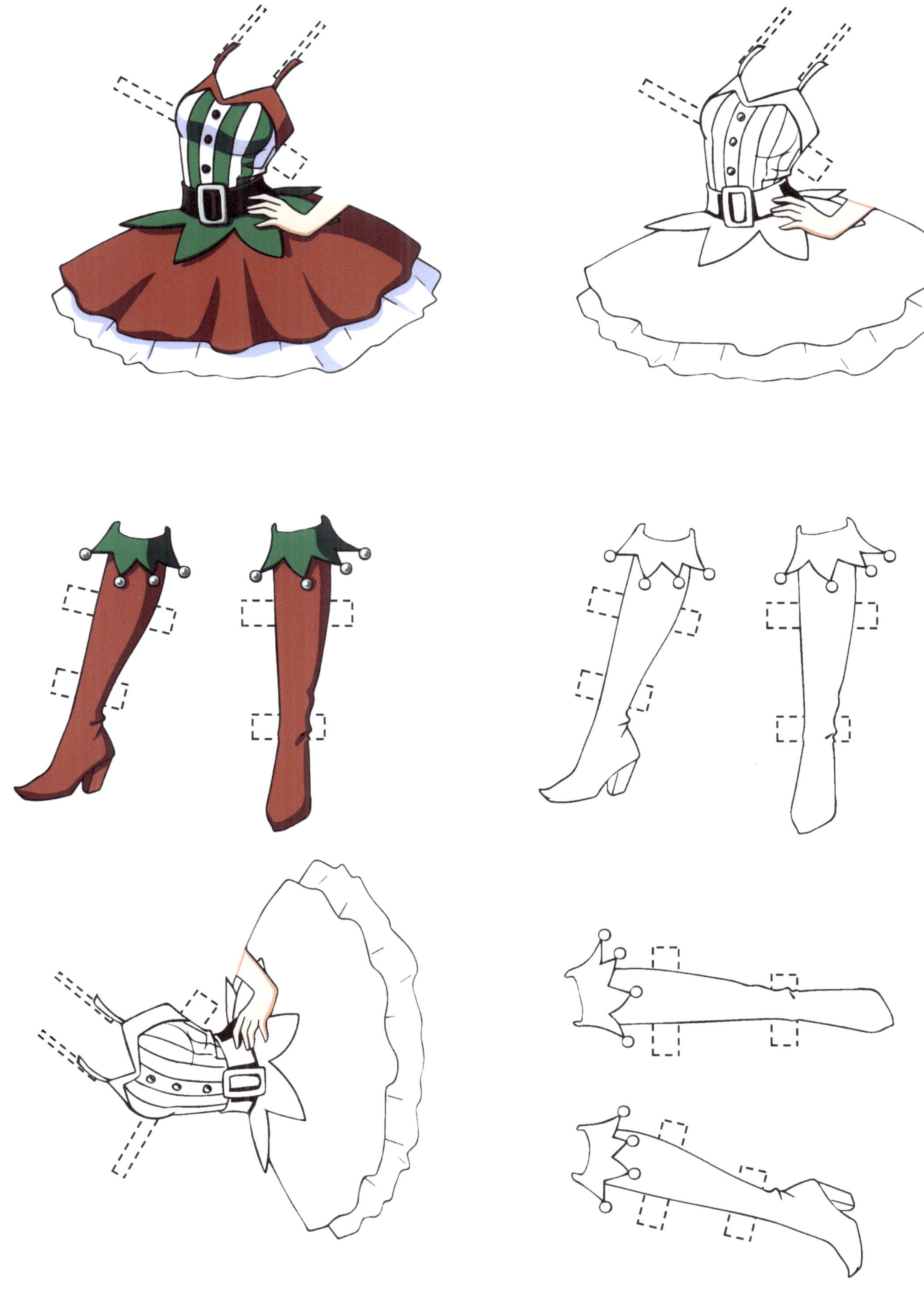

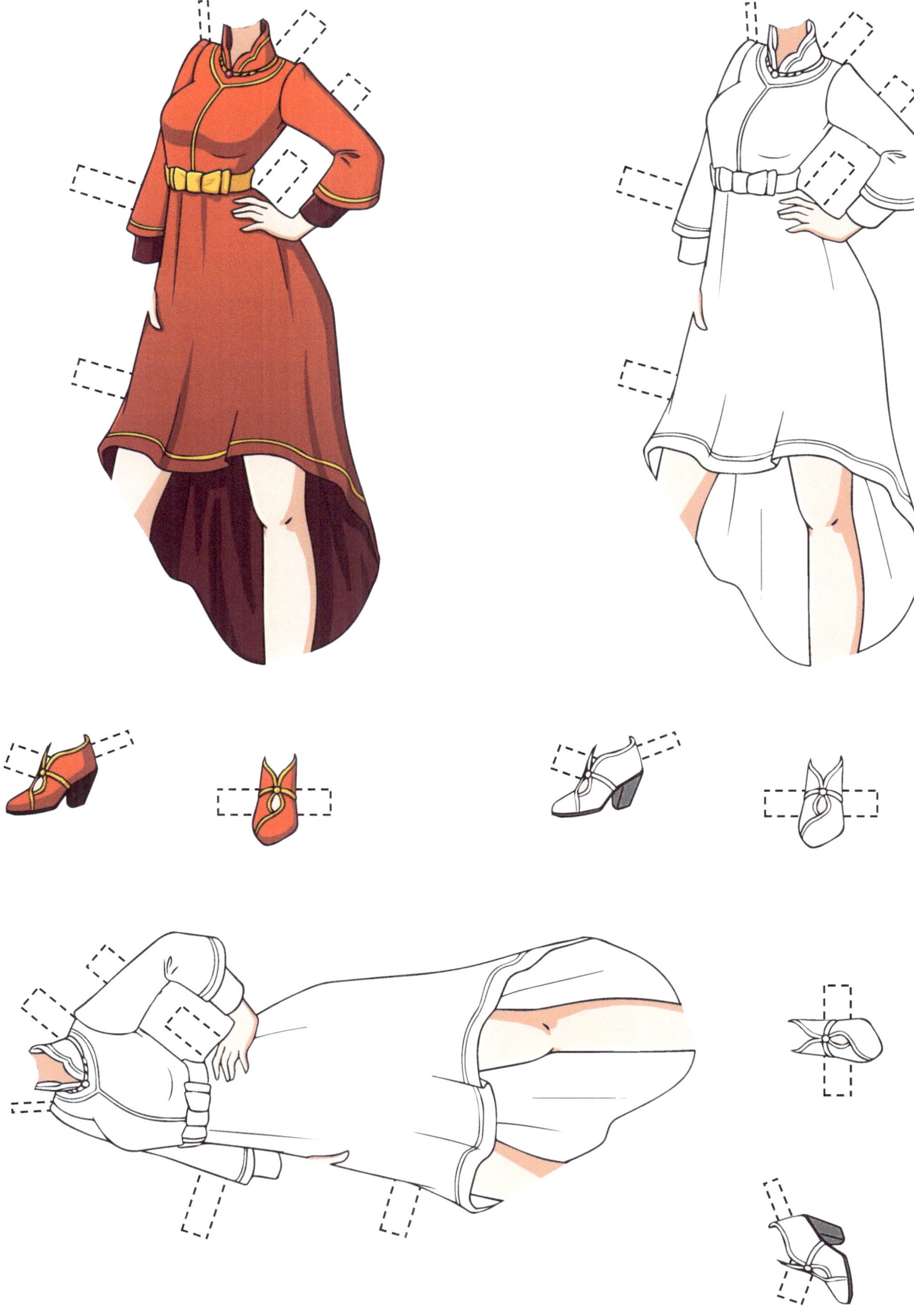

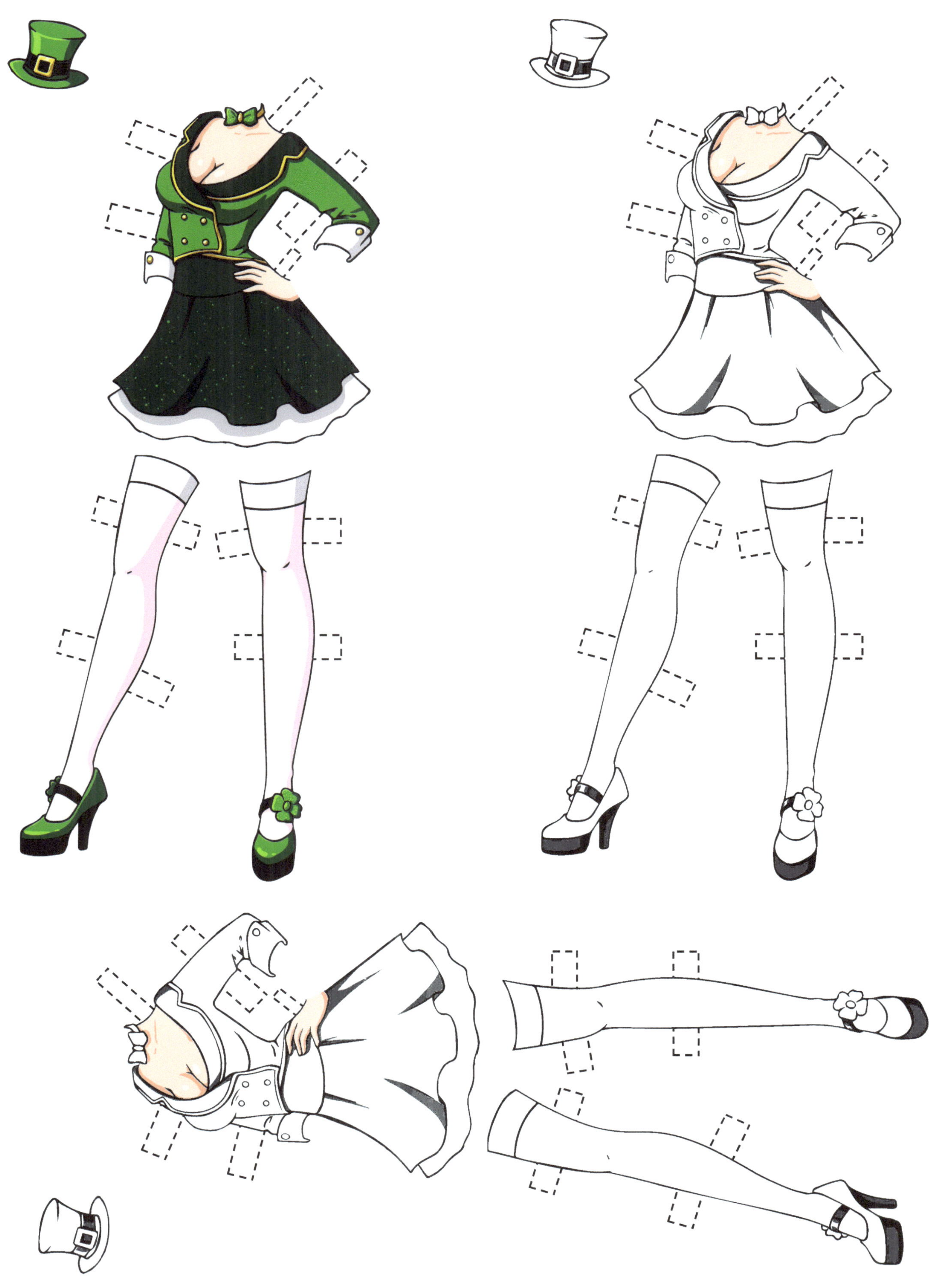

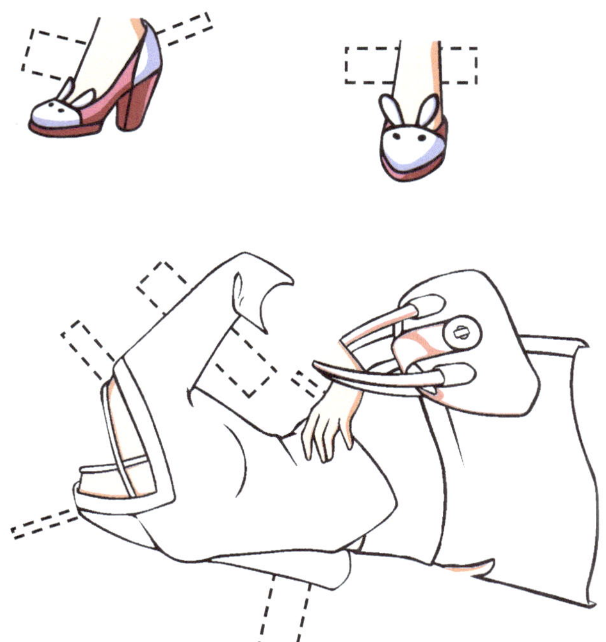
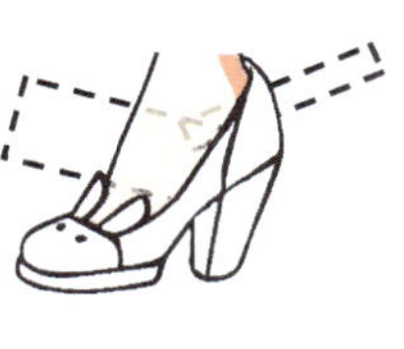
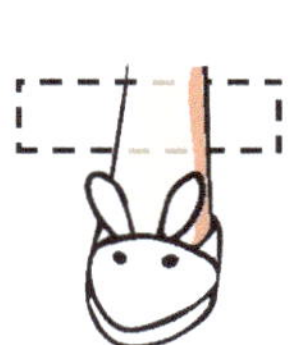
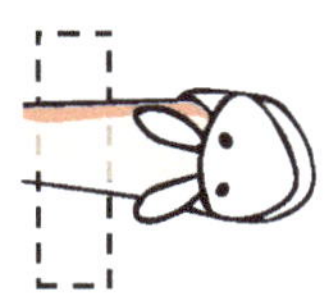

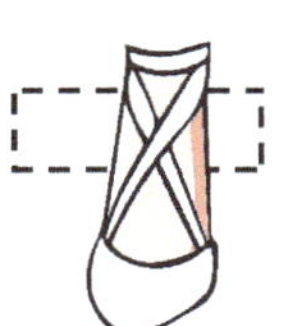
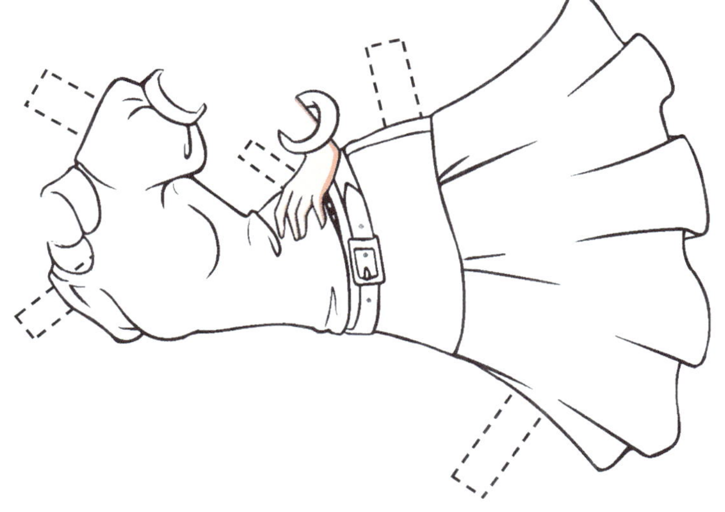
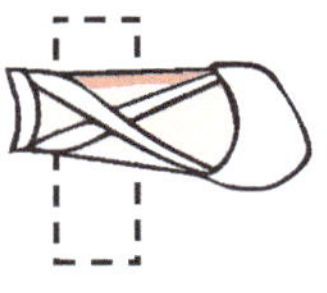

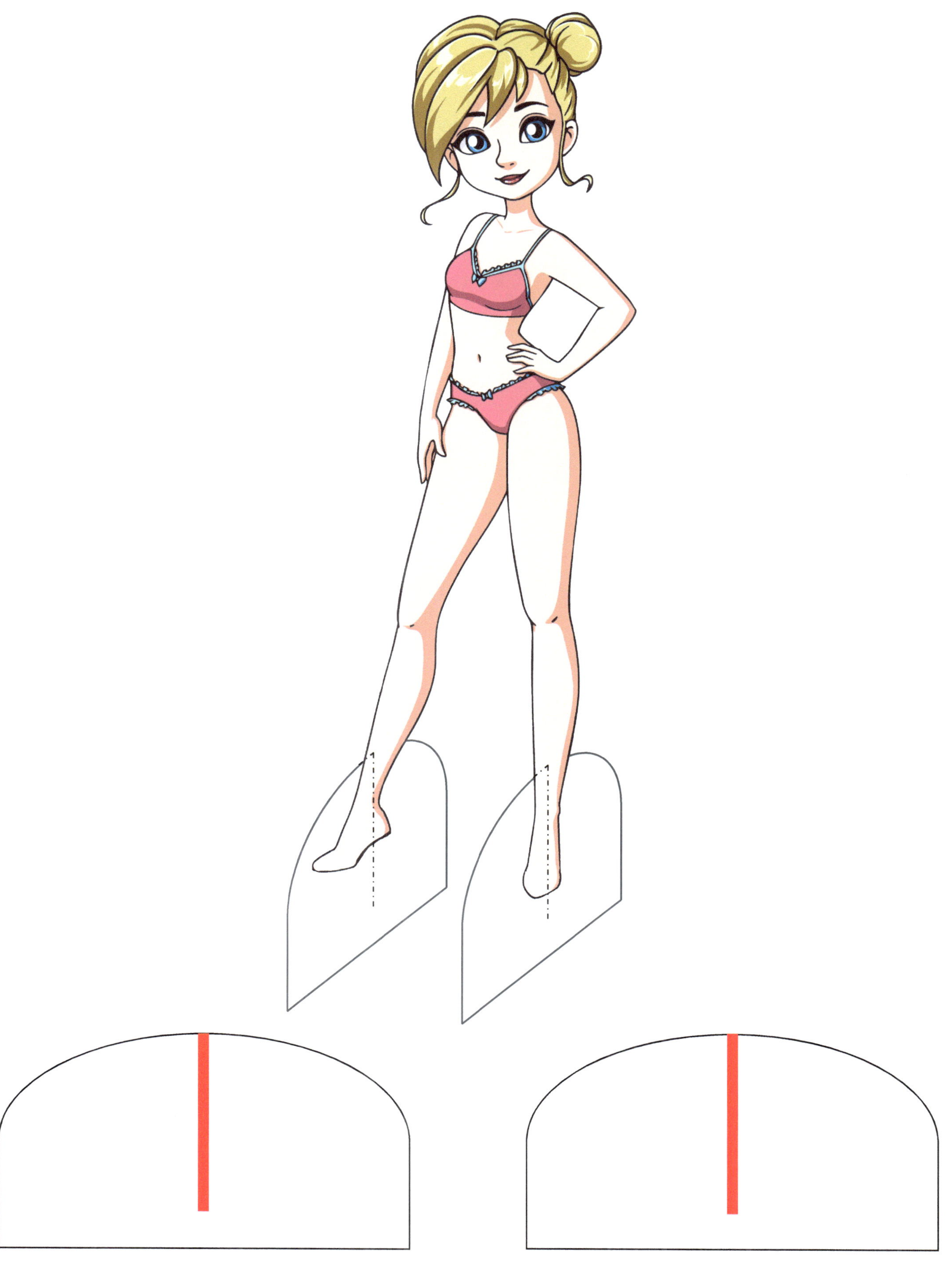